CW00384527

Afterlives

John Barnie

LEAF BY LEAF

Published by Leaf by Leaf
an imprint of Cinnamon Press
Office 49019, PO Box 92, Cardiff, CF11 1NB
www.cinnamonpress.com

The right of John Barnie to be identified as author of this work has been asserted by him in accordance with the Copyright, Designs and Patent Act, 1988. Copyright © 2021 John Barnie.

ISBN: 978-1-78864-925-4

British Library Cataloguing in Publication Data. A CIP record for this book can be obtained from the British Library.

All rights reserved. No part of this publication may be reproduced, stored in a retrieval system, or transmitted in any form or by any means, electronic, mechanical, photocopying, recording or otherwise without the prior written permission of the publishers. This book may not be lent, hired out, resold or otherwise disposed of by way of trade in any form of binding or cover other than that in which it is published, without the prior consent of the publishers.

Designed and typeset by Cinnamon Press.

Cinnamon Press is represented in the UK by Inpress Ltd.

Acknowledgements

Maurice Sochachewsky, *Their Burden* © Dave Skye, Peter Davies, *Tŷ Haf/Summer Cottage* © Peter Davies, both reproduced by kind permission.
Hugh Hughes, *Huw Griffith of Bodwrdda, with His Children* and *Richard Elis, Solicitor* reproduced by kind permission of the owners.
All other pictures by permission of Peter Lord.

Contents

Foreword

Peter Lord has been collecting paintings by Welsh artists for the past thirty-five years and during my friendship with him I have watched the collection grow into one of the finest in Wales. It is particularly rich in paintings from the nineteenth and early twentieth centuries.

Not long ago, I suddenly felt a need to write about them, and twenty-two poems wrote themselves in quick succession. Then they stopped, and that was that.

The poems are presented here alongside images of the paintings. They are not 'interpretations' in a narrow sense, but afterlives or alternative lives that sprang into my mind as I looked at the paintings again or retrieved them from memory.

Three of the paintings perhaps need a note of explanation. John Roberts's *Marquis of Anglesey*, twinned with the poem 'Pub Bore', has the appearance of an inn sign, but Peter is reasonably certain that in fact it hung on a wall inside the tavern. In 'The Lads', twinned with William Roos's *New Year's Eve*, 'the nude in the alcove' refers to a painted-out nude figure in the alcove at the right of the picture, which led me to an explanation of the severe expression on the maid's face as she holds out the candle on a rigid arm. William Roos's portraits *Woman in a Blue Dress* and *The Husband in Maroon* are of an unidentified husband and wife. The poem 'Eclipsed' refers back to the wife's portrait.

I am grateful to Peter for allowing the paintings to be reproduced in this way, and for supplying the images.

John Barnie

Afterlives

William Roos, *Walter Hussey de Burgh and His Daughter, Victoria*, 1850

OH, VICTORIA

What's that she's reaching up with under his chin
it's a tickling stone, very rare,
one stocking down, fancy blue ribbons

papa pretends to have fun, this
being a favourite daughter; he has power
and business too

easing her off his lap saying
your dolly is Welsh, we are not
though that is bye-the-bye.

William Jones Chapman, *Lady with a Flowered Bonnet*, 1839

NOUVEAU *AND* RICHE

I'm ready and here comes the painter upstairs
with paint pot and brushes
I did wonder plumes but Mr T said no
I'm best set off with flowers
'and display that brooch with rubies and gold';
he said the bodice was a French knight's armour
but that was his joke, it's soft as feather pillows;
I don't like the shine on my nose
but the lace is very good; I must ask the ladies
round to tea, 'oh yes, that's me
now how many sugars do you take?'

Maurice Sochachewsky, *Their Burden*, 1937

YOU, THE OUTSIDER

Churchill's in his club swapping Boer War stories
the police are all Tories
everyone knows that, picking nutty slack
off tips, the poor man's pyramids;

what are you staring at whose coal-shed
has the biggest lumps
veneered with fool's gold or
pressed with fossil ferns;

coal is heavy, life a hardship, sliding
over rustling slag to home,
watch the anger in the woman's eyes
as it follows you round the room.

Hugh Hughes, *Richard Elis, Solicitor*, 1813

SOLID

I've a long nose to look down
and never make jokes

but I have a name, ELIS, CYFREITHIWR,
the man to go to, opening a door

on my brown-painted room, sparse
as a vestry and me looking up

casually holding a thumb where
I'm mentioned in the *Gazette*.

Anonymous, *Poor Taff*, c. 1770–1820

TAFFY TROTS TO LONDON

Ninety-seven miles so still a way to go
with a leek cockade and a leek sword
and stink from the goat let it be known
driving him from town to town
    'on yer goat Taff

the goat looks angry and Taffy looks hurt;
    but that's the English for you

    —BORIS LAYS DOWN LAW TO EU—
(these foreign johnnies have to be told)

    as it was so it is now
but wait a minute, what does the Englishman ride
    if not a Berkshire pig.

Hugh Hughes, *Huw Griffith of Bodwrdda, with His Children*, 1813

HORRIBLE LITTLE BRATS

We didn't want to but Tada said we had to
so we sulked
'smile for the gentleman'
but we wouldn't
so he blotched our faces which wasn't fair
and made us stupid
'you'll never be beauties'
under his breath,
but we don't care, *WE DON'T CARE*.

Henry Clarence Whaite, *God's Acre*, 1865

WHAT WAS THE SERMON ABOUT?

Here they come crowding through the lychgate
Nain talking to the little girl who is glad to leave God's Acre
where tombstones lean toward each other and the dead sleep on;

the black dog by the way isn't an omen
he just came nosing about at the sound of voices;

home now to a roast dinner across the fields
the father permitted a jest, carving the meat;

you have to peer to see this through thick cracking varnish
like Capel Celyn when the lake evaporates,
the village laid bare in a crazy paving of mud.

John Roberts, Hen Walia, Caernarfon, *Marquis of Anglesey*, 1832

PUB BORE

By God, Sir, never bin in a cavalry charge?
let me tell you how it's done;
first the bugler signals 'Trot', then 'Canter',
until you raise the inverted sabre

'B r i g a d e ... C H A R G E';
damn me, Sir, nothing finer,
thunder of hooves, yelling of men,
white smoke from enemy cannon

pock and *suck* as grapeshot finds a home,
men pitching, horses screaming,
but on you go until, by God, Sir,
you're in among 'em cutting left and right,

damn me, slashed an arm clean off
at Waterloo; I was young then, by God;
reduced to hanging now on a tavern wall
but, damn me, Sir, I've lived, I've *lived*.

Archie Rhys Griffiths, *Miner Resting*, c. 1932

BARE

'Light at the end of the tunnel'
for you, not me; here I am
with a fashionable 'tache, 'resting'
the caption says, my body
not yet marked, so I could be a

street fighter with muscle,
hacking at black seams, but
I'm 'resting' not thinking,
you know nothing about me
can deduce nothing from this.

William Morgan Williams, *Humphrey Owen, Llety, Caernarfon*, 1860

RAZOR

He's sharp, make no mistake
keeps himself lean
I wouldn't ask for a kind word
or a loan

the backs of his hands are veined
there's sagging under the chin
women say he has a brown-eyed smile
or used to

it's sour-apple time now
and he dresses in black
two great wings of eyebrows
ready to take flight.

John Lewis, *Elizabeth Gwynne of Taliaris*, c. 1736-37

ROSEBUD

Little rosebud girl
how sentimentally sweet you are

the double rose of life held between finger and thumb

because of the thorns
rose her sash, rose her buckled shoes

may she never grow up
never lose her smile.

Evan Hugh Parry, Pwllheli, *He Being Dead, Yet Speaketh, Charles Haddon Spurgeon Preaching at the Metropolitan Tabernacle, London*, 1881

HE THINKS WHILE HE PREACHES

I look around at these wooden souls
how many will be saved when Jesus comes reaping
not many I fear
the Lord's granary is capacious
but few sheaves will be gathered
so much rotten corn left standing in the fields
and when I am called
what can I say before the Mercy Seat
you were dead Lord but I heard you speak
I lifted the burden of this great chapel on my shoulders
and yet I was a poor farmer
my scythe was too blunt
I sheared too near the skin
all these doubts I raise with myself in the long coffin-nights
I seem a grand man to them, one of the elect,
yet no vessel can contain
my questioning and fear.

William Roos, *Woman in a Blue Dress*, 1839

STUNNING

Do you like my pendant earrings
solid gold of course
and my shining black crimped hair
which took hours

you must have patience to be beautiful
and the blue satin of my dress
and my cool shoulders
warning you away from my lips.

William Roos, *The Husband in Maroon*, 1839

ECLIPSED

Why dressed in maroon and woolly black
with a sombre red sky to his left, the face kind
but weak so this fireside Napoleonic stance
fails to convince; I think it's the wife's

chill radiance who has chosen dawn beyond the pillar
to illuminate her alabaster shoulders; how
can he bear to contemplate her turned-away indifference;
he has that smile; he is loving to their child.

Hugh Hughes, *Bwlch Llanberis*, 1847

Y BWLCH

'The dog barked and the sheep
jumped over the wall' (*Nursery Rhymes
for Babes*); but in this painting
the focus is the delirium of standing still
like the man who watches and the man
travelling far behind who will never
catch up with the lady's coach, if
that is what it is, pulled by a horse

born to slavery, except we don't
call it that, and didn't then; humans
can be slaves, but the animals we
strapped to coaches, whipped before carts
are only the semi-sentient precursors
of the triumph of lorries and cars.

Evan Walters, *Courting*, 1927

WHAT HAPPENED NEXT?

The ample woman and the blackened man,
she asleep in his lap

he with a slack white hand
as if saved for something

but too tired now;
light has been stolen by the trees

though it shines on the house and the road;
behind them the watcher, hands in pockets,

he knows their game;
only little boy blue is sinuously alive

drawing the string of a homemade bow
ready to take down a bird

or even the sun.

Archie Rhys Griffiths, *On the Coal Tips*, c. 1928-32

AESCHYLUS IN ABERDARE

Here we go, a Welsh Greek chorus
but whose tragedy are they in? don't you know?
their own, these mothers, rough and bold,
bearing to the terraces below

the burden of themselves not coal;
look at the slag heaps, look at the sky;
these women will defy anything
that gets in their way, unstoppable rage

and grief, wearing the colours of the earth
the one with a shawl that might be used
      for mopping blood.

William Jones Chapman, *James Evans, Welshpool,* 1841

SUCH A SUNNY DAY

Do you know about Dead Sea fruit
the skin is glossy but the flesh is ash;

after the painter packed up and left
little master cracked his whip; all

he could see, one day, would be his;
but next year he died; his parents

reached up to harvest the fruit; how
tender the skin, how bitter the taste.

Edward Owen, *Self-portrait*, 1732

I SAY!

The peacock of painting
do call him that, he'd be pleased,
not a splash of paint on his blue velvet coat

the necktie supreme, the wig
slightly girlish with that elegantly, carefully
gathered twist over the shoulder;

fop, fop, the street boys would shout if they dared;
let them; he has work to do
painting his masterpiece—himself.

William Roos, *New Year's Eve*, 1854

THE LADS

Don't look at the midnight chimes of the mantlepiece clock
nor the maid holding out the bright candle of Truth on a rigid arm
the wine is good as is the painted-out nude in the alcove
she being their secret, though the disapproving maid has seen.

Archie Rhys Griffiths, *Miners Returning from Work*, 1928

DAY DONE

The clouds could be sails on one of Conrad's battered ships
if looked at right
storm-filled above this curiously still scene

where hands in pockets or walking with a crooked stick
they make their way to the terraces in shadow
for an evening shift with their wives.

Peter Davies, *Tŷ Haf/Summer Cottage*, 1984

ISN'T IT TIME?

Don't be alarmed we're perfectly tamed
bred to be servants
saying one thing thinking another
faces thresholds you never cross
because we don't let you—*gotta use words*—
but whose words
in Birmingham-on-Sea.